Negotiation Strategies and Tactics for Small Business

How to Lower Costs, Raise Sales, and Put More Money in Your Pocket.

Raging Zebra Publishing

Odessa, Florida

Table of Contents

Preface

I have been a serial entrepreneur for over 30 years, owning businesses, ranging from a dry cleaner to a computer software company. In that time, I haven't been able to find even one good book on negotiation that was written with the little guy in mind. There was just wasn't a good guide to negotiation for small business owner. There were few college classes available to teach students this necessary skill. I didn't take a class in negotiation until I was in graduate school, working on my MBA. Even then, it was offered only as an elective.

I decided to fill the gap. I read every book on negotiation that I could find (there are hundreds.) I read every article available in the financial press regarding commercial negotiations, going back years. I talked to dozens of people who negotiate for a living, people who sell cars, industrial equipment, commercial supplies, manufacturing component parts and wholesale inventory. Then I investigated the other side. I talked to professional buyers, who spend their days negotiating the best deals for their companies on the same thing these sellers were selling. Collectively, they had over 1,000 years of experience in negotiation.

I wanted to know the overall strategies and the specific tactics that I could use to do well negotiations. I wanted to know how to deal with all the ploys, gambits and dirty tricks that I might encounter.

I took the information that I gleaned from my research and distilled it here. In these pages is the gist of what I learned. Read it, use it, and always get a good deal.

Introduction

Every day we read about high stakes negotiations. The mergers of giant companies and heated negotiations between labor unions and employers are stories that show up in the financial pages. Salary talks between highly paid athletes and sports teams are reported in the sports section. Treaties between countries and negotiations that precede them fill large sections of the news.

Big companies or rich sports stars have paid negotiators doing their bargaining for them. But we have to do it ourselves. We have no highly skilled team of negotiators working on our behalf.

This book, is concerned with the kind of negotiation that's done by small business people in the course of the day's work. Small business people have to negotiate with landlords, suppliers, vendors, government regulators, employees, and customers, as well as a host of others.

Often we have to negotiate with others that seem to have the upper hand , big companies with clout, banks with their stacks of money and snooty attitudes, and slick salespeople well trained in the art of negotiation. You can learn the strategies and tactics of these practiced negotiators and no longer be at their mercy. You can hold your own and even come out ahead.

You may have bought a house or a car. You might have discussed your pay when you took a job. You have experience in negotiation but what you don't have is training. It's time to learn how to negotiate without more painful and expensive experience. It's time to learn from *other people's* painful and expensive experience.

Most books on negotiation are aimed at larger companies where they have teams of trained negotiators .They certainly have their place. But, this book is for you, the small business person.

If, for instance, you're buying a new piece of equipment priced at $5000,with 15 minutes of negotiation, you might get it for $4000. $1000 is certainly worth a few minutes time.

Or perhaps a valued employee is insisting on a big raise. You know he's worth it, but it will add up to a lot of money over time. While negotiating, you might find that the employee needs the money to pay a babysitter to watch his kids between the time that they get home from school and the time he gets off work. More flexible work hours might be more valuable to him than more money. If you can rearrange his work schedule so he gets home earlier, he'll probably be happy with less money than he started out insisting on. You save money; he gets a better work schedule. Everybody's happy.

The time and effort you spend at negotiation can pay for themselves many times over.

Chapter 1

Types of Negotiation

What is negotiation? Simply put, negotiation is a discussion aimed at reaching an agreement. Not all negotiations end in agreement, but that is their goal. We negotiate because we value things differently than others people do. We trade what we value less than they do for what we value more. This difference in how we value things is the key to negotiation.

Distributive negotiation - How to Slice the Pie.

Distributive negotiation is also known as zero sum negotiation or win-lose negotiation. The parties compete over the distribution of a fixed value; any gain by one party represents a loss to the other. In this case, each negotiator is *claiming value*.

Distributive negotiators see negotiation as the distribution of a fixed amount between them and you. The more they get, the less you get. Power plays, manipulation, and ploys are the name of the game here.

Integrative Negotiation -Making a Bigger Pie.

Integrative negotiation is also known as win-win negotiation. To integrate is to bring together or incorporate parts into a whole. The parties in an integrative negotiation integrate their needs into a deal that is to the advantage of both parties..

As a kid, you may have collected baseball cards. When you first acquire your cards, you have no control over what cards are in the package. In time, you are likely to have gotten several duplicate cards. But you might not have all the cards for your favorite teams or players. Another card collector may have duplicates of the cards you want, or merely value them less than you do for some other reason. You would trade the cards that you want less for the ones you want more. Each party would end up with a collection of cards that he values more than before the exchange. There is a reason they're called trading cards.

This simple example of trading baseball cards is an instance of integrating both parties' goals to create mutual advantage. The negotiators are *creating value.*

Integrative negotiators work to build a deal that makes both parties better off. It is in integrative negotiations that most of your gains will come.

Distributive negotiation is often used in conjunction with integrative negotiation. We create a bigger pie (create value) and lay claim to a share of that bigger pie (claim value.) Both parties come out ahead, that's good. If we come our more ahead than the other guy, that's even better.

Chapter 2

Single Issue Negotiations

Entry Prices, Limit prices, the ZOPA and BATNA too

Most single issue negotiations are concerned with price. The limit price is the lowest the seller is willing to sell for or the highest price that the buyer is willing to pay.

The entry price is the price the seller would like to get if he can. It is the highest price the seller thinks he can make a case for. The buyer's entry price is the lowest price that he can make a case for. Also keep in mind a goal price. You can make a case for your limit price, but don't expect to get it. You can *hope* to get it, but don't *expect* to get it. Your goal price is the price you expect to get. Set your goal optimistically, but set it reasonably so. Your goal is sometimes called your aspiration price.

Somewhere between the seller's limit and the buyer's limit is where the deal might take place. This is the ZOPA, the Zone Of Possible Agreement. Mind you, there isn't always an overlap between these prices. There may be no ZOPA.

The amount that the seller receives over his limit (minimum) price what economists call the seller's surplus. Likewise, what the buyer pays less than his limit (maximum) is the buyer's surplus. Together they are known as the negotiator's surplus.

Negotiation determines how the negotiator's surplus is distributed. There may be no surplus to split, or negotiations may not reveal the ZOPA and there might be no agreement. But we usually don't know that before we start negotiations, so we start on the assumption that there is a price we can both agree on.

The key is to try to get as close to the other party's limit price as possible, even though we don't know what it is. We could ask, but we're unlikely to get a forthright answer. Always assume that the entry price is not the limit price and that it leaves room for negotiation.

There is usually no way to know if an offer is at the other negotiator's limit. All offers should be treated as if there is another offer in reserve.

If you think the other negotiator is misleading you that his present offer is his limit price, press for more by saying something like "Come on, you can do better than that." or "I know you must be kidding."

At some point you may reach his limit price, but it's hard to know for sure. Often price concessions get smaller and smaller as you get close to the limit price. It's no guarantee though. The other negotiator may be using smaller and smaller concessions to encourage you to think you're nearing his limit price.

Anchoring and Bracketing

Conventional wisdom says that you should not be the first one to name a price. If you offer $5000 for a piece of equipment, for instance, that the seller was willing to sell for $4500, it's a problem. The seller will either take the offer before you change your mind, or reset his limit price to $5000 and try to negotiate higher

There is always a risk in being the first to name a price. However, preparation can minimize the risk. If you're selling a car, you can check on the internet to find the usual selling price for similar models. Classified ads would give you an idea of other's asking prices. Research on less widely traded items may be more difficult, but still worthwhile. Research can help you estimate the likely ZOPA - the range in which any possible agreement will occur. The time spent on preparation is usually well rewarded.

Anchoring is an attempt to establish a reference point. The first price named will often be the reference point from which negotiations are conducted.

As an example, answer these two questions about the population of Switzerland.

Is the population of Switzerland more or less than 40 million?

What is the population of Switzerland?

You probably guessed somewhere between 20 and 60 million. The first question put the figure of 40 million in your head. Most people use that number as an anchor for their estimate when they guess at the population. The population is actually a little below 8 million.

First offers in negotiation are important if they establish an anchor. The other party to the negotiations will usually adjust their expected price closer to the anchor price. Using specific numbers like $1012.50 rather than $1000 will encourage your counterpart to think in smaller numbers and therefore less distance from anchor you've established.

Have you ever wondered why stores will often prominently display outrageously priced merchandise in their window? They are anchoring. If you see the $1800 purse displayed on the way into the store, the $350 purse inside seems like a bargain. Tags at stores that have a higher price crossed out and a new lower price displayed make merchandise seem like a bargain, even if it isn't. "Compare at" prices are used everywhere, and they work. Since most people are unaware of the anchoring effect, its use can be very effective. So don't be afraid to be the first one to name a price.

If the negotiator for the other side makes the first offer, and it isn't close enough to the price that you want, laugh it off and say something like. "Let's be realistic and start again with something like (your entry price.)"

You may want to use a technique called bracketing. If one negotiator opens with position below your goal, you can reply with an offer that places your goal in between his opening position and yours. For instance, your goal price for a piece of equipment is $1500. The seller offers a price of

$1800. That's $300 over your goal price. You would offer $1200, $300 under your goal price. You don't expect to get it for that price, of course. As negotiations proceed and concessions are made by both parties, try to keep your goal at the midpoint between the offers presented. This often results in better deals than could have been made otherwise.

What's your BATNA?

You should consider your BATNA before you start negotiations. BATNA stands for Best Alternative To a Negotiated Agreement. If your negotiations go south, what would be your alternative? It might involve buying from someone else, at a slightly higher price than you hope to get in the current negotiations, or selling for a little less, if you're the seller. It's good to consider this ahead of time. Good alternatives outside of a negotiation increase your bargaining power. It doesn't hurt to let the other party know that you have alternatives, but don't be explicit about what they are. Negotiators know when their opponent is desperate for an agreement and will push for much more, knowing that you have little choice but to give in to their demands.

A good BATNA may give you the clout to press for more concessions from an opponent who wants you to stay in negotiations. So it pays to consider your BATNA before negotiations and improve it as much as possible. If you're planning to buy a car, check the price and availability of similar model. If you can't buy the one you want for a reasonable price, you know what the best alternative is. It never hurts to estimate your opponent's BATNA either. If you know what his alternatives are, you can estimate how hard you can push for concessions before he'll decide to walk away from negotiations and go with his BATNA.

It's easy to get caught up in the moment and try too hard to reach an agreement, especially after you've put a lot of work into it. Knowing your BATNA can keep you from accepting any deal that is too unfavorable. It can also keep you from rejecting a deal that you should accept.

Unbundling

Unbundling involves separating parts of an agreement to make several smaller bargains. For instance, if you're selling a car and the prospective buyer is stuck at a price of $200 less than you're willing to take. If you think the buyer is limited by the amount of ready cash available to him, you might offer to take payments. "If you pay the $6,700 that I'm asking, I'll accept $6,000 now and the final $700 in two payments, two and four weeks from today"

This may solve his cash flow problem by letting him get a paycheck or two before he has to finish paying for the car. It will at least change the single-issue negotiation into a multiple issue negotiation. Any time you can unbundle a single issue negotiation into several issues, you improves the odd of being able to enlarge the pie that you're going to be splitting. Multiple issues give you the possibility of trading across issues to maximize the value to both negotiators.

Chapter 3

Multiple Issue Negotiations

Negotiations that comprise multiple issues offer multiple opportunities for mutual gain. Integrative, (win-win), negotiations almost always have several issues to negotiate.

Multiple issue negotiations are more involved than are single issue negotiations. Previous discussions on BATNA, ZOPA, anchoring and bracketing still apply, as do opening, goal, and limit prices. Our positions on each issue, however, must be considered in conjunction with every other issue. How much are we willing to give on one issue to get what we want on another?

There are 4 or sometimes 5 steps to negotiation:

- Preparation,
- Discussion,
- Proposals
- Bargaining and Agreement
- (Often) Post Agreement Negotiations

We'll discuss each step in order.

Chapter 4

Preparation

The foundation for doing well in negotiation is good preparation.

The first step in preparation is to identify your interests and the other party's interests. What do you want out of these negotiations? What is it that you hope to gain or what problem do you hope to solve? What does the other party want? The other party must want something from you, or there would be no need for negotiations at all. Try to be general, but not vague. "We want to increase our profit," is vague. "We want to cut our supply costs by 10% and thereby increase our profit margin.", or "We want to decrease the downtime on our equipment to less than 3.8%." are better.

Define your goal and evaluate how realistic that goal is. Set your goal to be ambitious but not unrealistically so.

Research alternatives to an agreement in your negotiations. Decide what you best alternative is, your BATNA. Research may also give you some insight into what your opponent's' BATNA may be. It's important to get the best estimate of their BATNA too.

Prepare a list of issues and positions. Issues are items on your negotiation agenda that will help you achieve your overall interests. Positions are your opening and exit points on each issue. There may be sub issues related to any issue. For instance, if you're negotiating a lease, one issue may be the monthly payment. Sub-issues might be who pays property taxes, insurance and maintenance. On each of these issues there will be positions, both yours and the landlord's.

Make a list with your issues and positions on one side and the other party's expected issues and positions the other. Think carefully when listing the other party's issues and positions. You don't want to be surprised by them bringing up issues that you never considered and didn't plan for.

You can't negotiate interests, though you should always keep both parties' interests in mind. You can negotiate issues and positions to further your interests. Taken together, issues and positions are called tradables

Once your tradables are listed, it’s necessary to prioritize them. I recommend 3 or 4 categories-high, medium, low, and no value to us. Ok, you're asking "Why would you list tradable of no value?". Good question. A tradable may be of no value to us, but should be listed if it may be of value to the other party. Don't give anything away, trade for it.

Collect all the data that you can. Industry trade groups are great sources of data. The internet can be a goldmine of information. If you're buying or selling something, it's important to research the market. Who else sells similar products? What are their prices, terms, and warranties? What are the seller's reputations for reliability and service?

If you're negotiating with an equipment supplier about their warranty service and your goal is to reduce downtime, collect data on your current downtime. Calculate what that downtime costs your company. Are there industry averages for downtime?

The data that you collect can help you define your interests and set your goals more accurately. It can help you refine the list of tradables, both yours and your estimate of the other party's. It will also be useful to back up your side in any debate during the discussion part of the negotiations.

"The industry average warranty service call response time is less than half of your company's average time." A statement like that is hard to dispute, especially if the source of the data is reliable. Be ready to show the source of the data to back it up, even if its figures you collected yourself.

Examine Differences to Find Likely Trades

Negotiation hinges on trading what you value less than your counterpart for what you value more. Businesses differ in their attitudes, time constraints, resources, expectations, and risk aversion, among other things. Exploit these differences for potential tradables. For instance, a supplier with plenty of cash on hand may be willing to accept extended payments from a business with less ready cash, in return for a higher purchase price

Differences in risk aversion might lead one business to accept a lower payout from a joint venture in return for lower risk exposure.

Leverage

Leverage refers to the principle of using a small advantage, or perceived advantage, to gain a much larger benefit. Leverage can be used to multiply and focus power in a negotiation. The more it costs you to not have an agreement with the other party, the more leverage the other party has.

There are different kinds of leverage

Normative leverage applies to the influence norms or standards have on your position. It may be standard industry practice to give net 30 terms. It may be standard practice to give 5% discount of orders of a certain size. Normative leverage can also come from social norms. In the US and many other western countries, the notion of "Fairness" is a powerful one. Urging someone to do something because it's fair is a powerful argument.

Positive leverage comes from the ability to provide the other party with something they want, or reward them in some way. *Negative leverage* is just the opposite. It's the power to deny someone the thing they want, or to punish them.

The more it costs you to not have an agreement with the other party, the more leverage the other party has. Having a good BATNA lowers the cost of not reaching an agreement and decreases the leverage that the other party many have over you.

Your Relationship With the Other Negotiator

Consider whether you're going to have an ongoing relationship with the other party. Are you engaged in a single transaction and never expect to do deal with this business or person again? The stakes in this kind of negotiation are more important than the possibility of an ongoing relationship. Often, however, your relationship with your counterpart or the company he works for is important. It may be a supplier, a customer or an employee. You want a good deal, but you don't want to push for the last little bit if it is to the detriment of your ability to deal in the future. You shouldn't be a pushover, but keep in mind the balance between the stakes in current negotiation and the value of a future relationship.

The people you deal with regularly should have a positive attitude toward you and want you to succeed. An employee who believes that salary negotiations ended too much in your favor may decide that low pay should be rewarded with low effort. A long term supplier may not try very hard to keep you happy if negotiations leave him with little advantage compared with not doing business at all. A customer who feels slighted on a deal is very unlikely to become or stay a regular customer.

In some cases where your negotiating counterpart feels strongly that he was treated unfairly, downright sabotage may occur. There are endless ways that people you do business regularly can perform acts of sabotage, big and small, to even the score.

Chapter 5

Discussion

Discussion is the next step in negotiation. Some people call it debate, others call it information exchange. Most of your time in negotiations will be spent in this phase. During discussions you will disclose, obtain, withhold and analyze information. Yes, withhold. You don't want to put all your cards on the table right at the onset of negotiations.

During the discussion phase of negotiation, you are trying to convince your counterpart that Your positions are the correct ones. You will give reasons, share data and argue your positions.

It's good to start off with a little small talk. This lets the parties get acquainted and find any common elements in their lives.

"Oh, you went to Princeton? My nephew is going there now. He says that it's quite challenging." Such connections help to build a rapport. Almost any connection helps. People tend to trust other people that have similarities to themselves. They also cooperate more readily. Some small talk helps negotiators see each other as people rather than just their opponent.

An occasional sincere compliment goes a long way toward building rapport. Sincerity is the key. "Clearly, you've done your homework." sounds sarcastic if he really hasn't.

Listen for any indicators that the other party has inhibitions about making the deal. There may be something standing in the way of a deal that is not obvious.

I once witnessed a negotiation about the sale of a business. It was owned by a husband and wife. They had started the business 25 years earlier and now they were planning to sell it and retire early. During negotiations, they appeared to be quite flexible about the terms, transfer date and almost everything else except the price. They simply would not sell their business for less than $1 million under any circumstances. It seems that they had promised each other and themselves that they would sell the business as soon as they could get $1 million for it. The buyers thought that price was a little too steep, but by stretching payments over several years at a low interest rate and getting concessions on a number of other issues, they made it palatable and the deal was sealed.

Inhibitions may be strictly personal. The other party may be reporting to a boss or partner and not want to lose face by returning from negotiations with a mediocre result. Working together to come to a solution that creates a bigger pie can go a long way to giving you both something to be proud of

Saving face involves maintaining one's public image or dignity. Even if you hold all the cards and your advantage is overwhelming, discussions may bog down if you don't give your counterpart a way to save face.

Allow your counterpart to make concessions gracefully, without having to admit that he backed down. Sometimes a change in wording or an exchange of minor tradables will help negotiators maintain their dignity, even when they are actually giving in very significantly.

Always give your counterpart a way to save face. At the conclusion of negotiations, congratulate him on a job well done. And never gloat, for heaven's sake.

Through all phases of negotiation, be alert for anything that may inhibit your counterpart's willingness to deal and address it as directly as you can.

Withholding and Disclosing Information

Negotiators should be truthful in negotiations, but that doesn't mean that you have to disclose everything. Selective disclosure, knowing what information to disclose and what to withhold, is useful negotiation tactic. Avoiding answering a direct question can be difficult. It's necessary to keep the perception of being honest and candid. A simple refusal is sometimes the only way to avoid answering. But consider the inferences your counterpart will make if you simply won't answer. A question like "How much profit are you going to make on this deal?" is certainly a question that you don't need to answer. A vague answer like "Enough to make it worthwhile, but certainly not enough that I can retire early." will answer the question without actually answering it and doesn't have the same effect as outright refusal.

Deflecting a question can be done in several ways. Answer a question that was not asked, acting as if it was the one asked. Politicians love to do this.

Another option is to appear ignorant of the answer. You can also disagree with any assumption that the question makes. This is another favorite of politicians. "Do you think increased government spending will halt the economy's slide into recession?." "I don't think the economy is sliding into a recession..."

While you don't want to tell everything you know, don't needlessly withhold information that might help your counterpart understand your interests. Your counterpart may reciprocate by being more forthcoming with information than he otherwise would. Many books on negotiation advise you to play your cards close to your chest and not reveal any more than is needed. That is an impediment to the search for win-win solutions. If both parties are well informed of each other's interests, the search will be widened. More and better possibilities for mutual gain can be considered.

Remember that while you're being open with the other negotiator, be judicial with what you revel and how you word it. Say something like "The extra working capital from this loan will help us expand into new, lucrative markets." Don't say "If we don't get this loan, we might as well just close up shop and go home."

Handling Disagreement

Disagreements aren't unusual in negotiations. They are best handled by asking questions and exploring the roots of the disagreement. Be sure to consider the possibility that you are wrong. Above all, don't try to force the other negotiator to admit that he is wrong. Identify the inhibition behind the disagreement so that you can find a way to work around it. Sometimes just acknowledging a disagreement will help. Perhaps the matter not in agreement can simply be passed over. Diplomats often will propose a simple agreement such as "If you don't shoot at us, we won't shoot at you." They will dispense with blame and incriminations in an effort to get right to an agreement that benefits both sides. It's important to remember that you can't negotiate someone else's beliefs or principles.

Behavior of Skilled Negotiators

Destructive Behaviors to Avoid

You should, at all times, be civil, even cordial. These are business discussions, try to remain objective. Above all, don't be irritating. A couple of researchers, Neil Rackham and John Carlisle, did a study regarding the behavior of successful negotiators compared with those who were less successful. Successful negotiators avoided destructive behaviors. Specifically:

Threatening

"If you don't pay us what we want, we'll go on strike!" "Fine, go on strike. We'll fire the lot of you. There are plenty of people who would love to have your jobs!"

Threats rarely work. Threatening the other negotiator is not a good way to ensure his cooperation in seeking win-win solutions. Most people don't respond well to being threatened. It's likely that they will dig in their heals to make it clear that they will not be swayed by your threats. Counter threats are also likely, which can provoke counter-counter threats and so on. Negotiation ends and deadlock ensues.

Attacking or blaming.

"These talks would have been done by now if you weren't so stubborn." Attacking the other party just puts him on the defensive. This may lead to defensive behavior or counter attacks. Arguing about who is to blame for what sidetracks the negotiations and leaves bad feelings all around.

Blocking

"Our payment terms are set. They can't be changed. There's no use even talking about it." Blocking stops any discussion before it can start. It takes the whole subject off the table. If someone does this to you, question him on why he blocked the subject.

Interrupting

Nobody likes to be interrupted. Besides being impolite, it's irritating. If someone is saying something that you don't agree with, wait until they're finished, then politely disagree.

Point scoring

Point scoring refers to any remark that insults or attacks the other party in a way that you might consider clever or humorous. Keep your witty repartee to yourself and negotiations will go much more smoothly. It may seem amusing to you but it won't be at all entertaining to the target of your remarks. Resist the urge.

Assertions and assumptions

"Clearly you're trying to blame the workers for the financial difficulties of the company." Assertions or assumptions about the other party's motivation, stance on issues or position are counterproductive and can take a long time to correct. Even if they are correct, the other negotiator might not want to admit it.

Helpful Behaviors

Rackham and Carlisle found that successful negotiators use the following:

Neutral statements

Neutral statements are used share information with the other negotiator. They are not aggressive or accusatory. Neutral statements can be used to volunteer information or ask questions. You can share information on your views and attitudes, as well as factual information. The most important part of the discussion phase of negotiation involves this exchange of information.

The important thing here is to keep the statement neutral. "We had to suspend production 3 times in the last 2 months because of delayed arrival of parts." Rather than "We had to suspend production 3 times in the last 2 months because you were late delivering parts." By using a neutral statement, the parts delays become a problem that can be solved by the cooperation of both parties. Otherwise, it's just an accusation and an effort to lay blame and might elicit a response like "Your parts weren't there because you didn't give us nearly enough notice of the change in specifications." This could result in a vicious circle of attacks and blame. All the while nothing is being accomplished.

Neutral statements are part of an effort to get the other party see our point of view. We use them to persuade the other party and encourage them to see things from our standpoint.

Assurances

Let the other party know that your intentions are to find a mutually beneficial conclusion to negotiations. Occasional comments reflecting you positive attitude are useful in setting the tone of the negotiations. "We're making good progress here." "Working together, we're both going to come out ahead." "I'm confident that we can make a deal here."

Questions

Questions can be used to verify assumptions. In the preparation stage you made your best estimates about the other parties' interests and priorities. By asking questions we can encourage the other negotiator to disclose enough information to assess the accuracy of those estimates.

We may also be able to gather information about what reservations the other party has about any part of the agreement we are trying to hash out.

Questions help draw out information from the other negotiator. If you ask "What's the absolute lowest price you'll sell for?" you probably won't get a straight answer. If you ask "How much of a discount could you give for a volume purchase?" you might get you a more straightforward answer. Open ended questions invite elaboration from the other party.

When asking questions, start with broad, general questions. A simple "How's business?" will often elicit a more complete response than you might expect, especially if you encourage it by looking like you're interested in what your counterpart is saying. A nod or a "hmm..." at the appropriate moment will encourage him to keep talking. General, open ended questions will often draw long answers and elicit useful information. Further questions can get increasingly more specific.

Some negotiators will ask questions that they already know the answer to in order to judge the veracity of the other negotiator.

Summarize

This is a good way to see both parties are on the same page. Paraphrasing, we summarize what the other negotiator has told us. This invites the other party to correct any errors in your understanding and to summarize what he understands about what we have said. "So, if I understand correctly, you'll give us the price of $3.12 per unit as long as we order at least 1000 per month." "Yes, at terms of net 15 days.

Signaling

Signaling involves hinting at a softening of one's stance without making a proposal or obligating oneself. It invites further exploration of the issue. A statement like "We *normally* can't have pizza ovens delivered and installed that quickly." invites questions about the circumstances under which they can be delivered and installed that quickly.

Signals usually use words or phrases that mitigate the absolute nature of the statement.

"We *have little leeway* to deviate from the price list."

"*It's not our policy* to extend free technical support for more than 90 days."

"The *standard* warranty is 1 year."

"Shipping is *generally* FOB, Cleveland."

"There are *few circumstances* that would cause us to deviate from our usual terms.

These all invite questions intended to open wider discussion.

Listening

Everybody knows how to listen. But listening well takes practice. It's too easy to split our attention between what someone is saying and our own internal thoughts.

You may be thinking about what you going to say next. You're just waiting for the other guy to quit jabbering on so you can say something *important*.

It's easy to let your mind wander while someone else is talking. But don't do it. Pay close attention. This takes practice, it really does. But without careful listening it's easy to miss the subtleties in what the speaker is saying. When signaling, the phrasing and the hedging phrases are easy to miss if you are not paying close attention.

Don't hesitate to take notes. If you want to ask a question about what your counterpart is saying, but don't want to interrupt, make a note of it and ask when he's done. People rarely object it you take notes while they are speaking. It is a clear indication that you're paying careful attention.

Negotiation writer Richard Shell suggests that you imagine that you've taken up skydiving. You are preparing for your first jump the instructor is telling you how to fold your parachute. He is only going to tell you once, he won't repeat himself. You will be depending on your chute opening properly when you pull the ripcord a short time from now. How closely would you listen to that instructor?

During the discussion phase of the negotiation, it would be wise to amend or correct the list of tradables that you made earlier. You may have found out that your counterpart's positions are not exactly what you expected. You may need to adjust your thoughts on the other negotiator's priorities on some issues. You might even need to reconsider priority and positions regarding your own tradables.

Chapter 6

Proposals

A proposal is a tentative movement toward an agreement. It is a statement suggesting a way to move negotiations forward, closer to agreement. A proposal is more direct than a signal.

Making a Proposal

A good proposal consists of a condition and an offer. It should be spoken in a confident tone of voice, avoiding the rising tone that might signal uncertainty. It should not be phrased as a question.

"If you will.... Then we will ....." rather than" Will you... if I...?"

A proposal should use assertive language. Don't be wishy-washy.

"I need" rather than "I would like."

"I expect" rather than "I hope"

Proposals are tentative, but become increasingly less so. The condition can be either vague or specific, but the offer is always vague. This encourages further discussion and counter proposals. It helps clarify each party's needs and each iteration of a proposal should get us closer to agreement. A negotiator who only makes an offer is giving things away. A good negotiator never gives anything away without getting something in return. Hence the phrasing, it should always state the condition (what you want), and then the offer (what you will give).

"If you accept our price, we can discuss a larger order."

"We must insist on a 1 year warranty, but in return we'll accept shorter terms for payment."

"If you will cover installation costs, I will consider purchasing more than one unit."

"If you accept the flexible terms we asked for, we could consider making you our sole supplier"

The condition should always be specific. The offer can be vague or specific. As we get closer to agreement, the offer will likely get more specific. Stating a proposal should be direct and to the point.

Keep it short. State the condition, the offer, and then wait for the response.

Receiving a Proposal

If you are on the receiving end of a proposal, don't interrupt. The other party might not understand the value of brevity. Listen to the whole proposal. Make notes if necessary. When the proposal is done, fell free to take a moment to think about it before responding. Don't immediately make a counterproposal. An immediate counterproposal would make it seem as if weren't listening carefully. Ask questions about the proposal. Get more specifics, clarify the details and invite your counterpart to expand on the proposal.

If it's not a very simple proposal, summarize it to make sure you understand it. Again take a moment to consider what benefit the proposal would give you and what it would cost you. Then you can state what you like and don't like about it. Tactfully of course. Use the positive behaviors listed in the chapter on discussion-making neutral statements, giving assurances, asking questions, summarizing, signaling, and careful listening

Be noncommittal, now might be the right time to make a counterproposal. Don't hesitate to bring in other issues; it's often useful to link other issues in your counterproposal. Keep an eye on the complete bargain and don't limit yourself to one issue at a time. You're trying to clarify your understanding of what issues are more important and less important to the other negotiator.

Summarize the proposals. Do it out loud. Write them down. If there is a blackboard or a whiteboard where they can be written for all to see, that's even better. Include proposals whether they have been agreed to or not. This will make it clear where each negotiator stands on each issue and prepare the road for the bargaining phase.

Chapter 7

Bargaining and Agreement

Bargaining

We're nearing the end of negotiations now. It's time to get more specific. In this phase you will make your bargains. A bargain consists of a specific condition and a specific offer. Vagueness and ambiguity are a thing of the past. A bargain removes the tentativeness from a proposal. They will often grow from the proposals discussed earlier.

"If you will take $1.46 per unit we will agree to buy 30,000 over the next 12 months."

"If you will give us an additional 6 months parts and labor warranty, we will pay a 10% deposit, 40% on delivery and the rest as soon as the unit it up and running."

"If you will cover installation costs, we'll purchase three."

These are simple bargains, often it gets much more detailed. Links between tradables are the order of the day. Bargains made now are provisional. The deal is not complete until the whole deal is complete. Some bargains made may need to be revisited during the course of negotiations. Don't hesitate to make this clear to the other negotiator.

Since you'll be linking tradables it will be necessary to keep track of several tradables at once.

This can be a messy affair, but if you try to confine your bargains to one issue at a time, you'll miss your best chance at a win-win solution to the negotiation. Linking one issue with another allows you to trade what you value less for what your counterpart values more. That's the whole gist of integrative bargaining. It's how we create value.

Effective negotiation involves the linking of one tradable to another using movement on one to secure movement on another. Movement on one tradable may be linked to the other party's movement on two or three other tradables. Creativity pays dividends here. Consider all the possibilities for linkage.

An example would be buying software for your business. Some tradables might be:

Price

Training

Tech support

Installation

No doubt, there will be more tradables, but these are a few main ones. A bargain in these circumstances might be "If you include installation, training and tech support, we will pay your asking price."

A counter offer might be "If you pay our asking price, we will walk your IT department through installation, train them to provide tech support to your employees and provide tech support for any question your IT department can't answer."

Don't try to reach agreement on issues in any specific order. That might be neat and tidy, but the price for such organization is a less than optimal agreement. Again, value is created by trading something you value less than your counterpart for something you value more. This exchange of one tradable for a different one, in search of an optimal agreement is often referred to as the negotiation dance. Don't negotiate issues sequentially, negotiate issues simultaneously.

There is an often told story (at least by negotiators) about two cooks who argue over the last orange in the kitchen. After some argument, they decide to cut the orange in half and each chef gets half. Neither got all he needed for his recipe to turn out well. Later they discovered that one chef's recipe called for using the peel and the other chef's called for the juice. Simply splitting the orange resulted in a less than optimal result. If they had taken the time to explore the possibilities, both would have gotten all they wanted. (Sometimes this story includes egg yolks and whites instead of orange peels and juice. Negotiation trainers seem to have a fixation with food.)

Perfectly fair agreements exhibit what economists call Pareto optimality. Pareto was an Italian economist who developed a concept of economic efficiency. In negotiations, a Pareto optimal outcome is one such that no one could be made better off without making someone else worse off.

How far you want to go to make yourself better off (even if it means makes the other party worse off) is another question. It depends on what kind of on-going relationship we expect to have with the other party.

Remember, when negotiating, do not give anything away. Even if it has no value to you, it may have value to the other party. Trade for something you want.

Summary and Agreement

Despite our best effort, sometimes an agreement can't be reached. If at some point, you have moved all you are willing to move on the issues and any more concessions would put you in a position inferior to your BATNA, it may be time for the take it or leave it ultimatum. Summarize out loud or in writing where everyone can see what has been agreed, and what has not. State the best you are willing to do, from your counterpart's view and simply tell them that that's the best you can do. Make it clear, without being adversarial or confrontational about it, that this is your final offer and that you hope that they will take it. It may help to offer them time to think it over. Limit the time you give them to decide. You don't want to lose your best alternative to a negotiated agreement by dilly-dallying. You also don't want them to think that they can delay until you have no alternative. Maybe they will take your final offer and maybe they won't.

If you're close to an agreement, but discussions have stalled, it may be worthwhile to take a break and adjourn discussions until a later time. This is a risky option. Your counterpart may think of reasons to not go through with the deal or to reopen issues that you thought were already agreed upon. But it also gives you and the other negotiator time to consider previously unexplored means of solving the problems that are stymying negotiations. Either of you may come up with a new way of making the pie bigger or overcoming each other's inhibitions. Before the adjournment, summarize the negotiations so far. Put down on paper what has been agreed to so far and what has not. Each negotiator should have a copy.

Contingent agreements are used when negotiators cannot agree on the state of future conditions or future occurrences. For instance, a supplier thinks that an ice cream store's estimates of future sales are too optimistic. The ice cream store's owner doesn't agree and want's a larger quantity discount based on sales. The supplier may ask the store owner to pay the standard price, but offer a quarterly rebate to the store owner if his sales (and therefor, orders from the supplier) are over a certain amount.

Contingent agreements can also be used as an incentive. It's common for builders to get bonus if they complete a project before the agreed upon date. They usually have penalties for finishing late. If a city is widening a busy road, traffic will be even more snarled while construction is ongoing. Finishing quickly will reduce the time frustrated commuters have to endure the traffic slowdowns and cut down on the angry calls to city hall.

For contingent agreements to work, both parties must have similar interests. The incentive must be to the benefit of both parties. In the ice cream store example, both the store owner and his ice cream supplier want high sales. There must also be clear agreement on how the terms of the agreement will be measured, the quantity of ice cream purchased in the previous quarter, for instance.

If an agreement has been reached on all the issues at hand, we need to put it in writing. Review the details, write them down and make a copy. Both negotiators should sign both copies and each should take one.

If this is a sales transaction, you may be using a pre-printed form. Make sure the details are on the form and that any preprinted conditions on the form either apply or are crossed out. The hard to read fine print on the back of the forms counts too. It's legally binding under most circumstances. Take the trouble to negotiate it or cross it out.

A more formal agreement may require a lawyer to draw up a contract. Have him use the previously written agreement that you both signed as a guide. Be careful about letting you lawyer complicate things. Part of their job is to try to protect you from every eventuality, but if they draw up a contract that deviates in any significant way from your negotiated agreement, you may be back at the negotiating table starting at square one. Remember that a contract is only as good as the people signing it.

Chapter 8

Post Agreement Negotiations

Finishing the Details

Even the most carefully crafted agreement leaves something out. Sometimes that's intentional. You might come to an agreement involving the general principles but leave the details to a later date. It might be left to the lawyers to hammer out legal details, or for the engineers to deal with the technical specifics

Most of the time, a small business doesn't have large teams of people with the specific expertise to do this type of negotiating for us. If an engineer's input is needed, you bring him to the negotiations with you. Run things past a lawyer if there are sticky legal questions or ask him to redraft an agreement that has been made to make it a legal contract. However, do most of the actual negotiating yourself.

Usually you are just dealing with minor things that come up after the agreement is settled. Production might find it can work more efficiently if a small change is made to a production part from a vender. A retailer may find that he is selling more of your product in blue rather than yellow and wants you to change the proportion of each color that you send.

Cooperation is the name of the game here. You and your counterpart have a working agreement. Assuming that neither of you are looking for an excuse to break that agreement, it pays to be flexible. If it would cost you 2 cents per part to change your production line to make a minor redesign in a part the other uses in production, tell your counterpart that you'll make the change for 2 cents per part. Explain that that's exactly how much more it will cost you. If that's an insignificant amount compared to the total cost, don't even mention it, just do it.

Sometimes repeated requests for little things can add up. One thing might be insignificant, but added together may be enough that the agreement needs to be modified to account for them. If both parties are happy with the original agreement, negotiating small changes to the agreement will usually be easy.

Sustaining the Agreement

Agreements don't last forever. Times change and the conditions that led to the agreement in the first place may no longer be valid. Agreements are sustained as long as both parties see more advantage to continuing the agreement than to breaking it.

A binding contract has legal consequences involved in breaking the agreement. These must be taken into account before breaking the contract. The higher the cost of breaking the agreement, the more binding it may be.

There is always the matter of reputation. A business that has a reputation for breaking contracts will have a hard time finding businesses that want to deal with it.

When constructing an agreement, take care to anticipate later difficulties. Nobody can foresee every eventuality, but it is worth the effort to try to predict the most likely problems and deal with them ahead of time. Contingencies and flexibility built into an agreement can sustain the agreement when complications arise. This may make the agreement more complex, but it can also keep it in force, to the benefit of both parties.

Renegotiating the Agreement

Some agreements are meant to be renegotiated: leases have a fixed term, employment contracts are expected to be renewed at some future date, supply contracts are renegotiated periodically. It is important to take into account the changes that the future will bring and to understand that not all changes can be predicted. Agreements of limited term are made with that in mind.

It is sometimes necessary to renegotiate when conditions cause an agreement to be very one sided, even if the agreement isn't set to expire. Recently in the U.S. many house owners sought to renegotiate their mortgages when the economy tanked and the prevailing interest rates dropped significantly. Lenders were reluctant to renegotiate to a lower rate, but had to consider the cost of the loan going into default and having to foreclose on the mortgaged property. There were lots of houses that were foreclosed on, and then sat empty for months or years, giving no return to the lenders at all. Sometimes it's wiser to renegotiate an agreement than to play hardball.

Chapter 9

Negotiator Styles

Givers, Takers, and Traders.

There are three basic styles of negotiators, givers, takers and traders. Givers are negotiators who consider negotiation strictly collaborative. They consider negotiations to be an exercise in joint problem solving. There's nothing wrong with that attitude, unless it's taken to the extreme. A giver who values agreement above all else may end up making too many concessions. By trying too hard to avoid conflict, he may end up on the losing side of a very one-sided agreement. This can lead to resentment and reluctance to fulfill the terms of the agreement.

Takers are negotiators who consider negotiations strictly distributive. They consider negotiations to be a struggle over who gets more of the pie. There isn't any thought about using integrative bargaining to make a bigger pie. Takers want to enlarge their share and don't care that getting more for themselves means that you get less. If there is any negotiator's surplus, they want and intend to get it all for themselves.

Traders are negotiators that take neither the giver nor the taker style to the extreme. Traders use both giver and taker styles of negotiation to achieve an optimal result. A trader is willing to give his counterpart something of value in return for something of value. This is the basis of the bargain. If you give me something, then I'll give you something. Traders invariably are the best negotiators.

Difficult Negotiators and Piano Playing Chickens

Sometimes you'll run across a negotiator who is demanding, loud, aggressive, unreasonable and just a real pain to deal with. These people are extreme taker style negotiators who think shouting, banging their fist on the table and general bad behavior will get them what they want. The problem is that sometimes it does. People who are intimidated by such tactics will often say "Sure, sure, whatever you want. Just go away." or something to that effect. Many people will simply avoid dealing with them. But, sometimes we have to deal with them.

When a difficult negotiator has a tantrum, treat it just as you would when a child has a tantrum, just ignore it, wait it out. Under no circumstances should you reward such behavior. If the difficult negotiator is rude and obnoxious, avoid the temptation to behave in like manner. Be polite, if he interrupts, wait until he finishes talking and even listen to him. Yes, it can be difficult, but remember to stay calm and polite. Don't forget the useful behaviors discussed in chapter 5, make neutral statements, give assurances, ask questions, summarize, and signal.

Chickens can be taught to play a tune on a toy piano by giving them tasty rewards that lead them to peck first on the correct key, then the correct sequence of keys. There are things that your obnoxious counterpart wants, or he wouldn't be at the negotiating table. Listen to discover what he wants and the interests behind his ranting and raving. Make proposals in the usual way, first the condition, then the offer. It may take several tries before you get it out without being interrupted. You may end up sounding like a broken record. That's OK. You're offering a reward if he will agree to the condition. That reward is like a tasty spoonful of chicken feed. If the first proposal gets no response, try another. Proposal by proposal, bargain by bargain, you are teaching your counterpart to negotiate in a civil manner, just like a chicken learning to play "Mary Had a Little Lamb."

As usual, when dealing with a difficult negotiator, don't give anything away. Make your counterpart trade for what he wants. Under no circumstances should anything be given to the obnoxious negotiator just to placate him. That would be rewarding and encouraging the difficult behavior. That behavior may have worked for him in the past, do not let it work with you.

Disputing Styles

Sometimes after an agreement has been made, disputes will occur over one party's fulfillment of its terms or in the interpretation of the agreement.

Jeanne Brett, Steve Goldberg and William Ury developed a theory of disputing styles is called the

Interest, Rights and Power model. It focuses on the different processes people use to deal with conflict, classifying approaches to conflict as being interest-based, rights based or power based.

Interests are the needs or wants that each negotiator wishes to have satisfied. Interests are the grounds for issues and positions in negotiations. Interest based negotiators try to focus on underlying interests of the parties by looking past the demands. By identifying and recognizing underlying interests the parties are encouraged to see their disagreement as a common problem that they must work together to solve.

Rights are independent standards of fairness or legitimacy: norms, customs, rules, legal rights, or standard industry procedures. A rights based negotiator invokes these rights to pressure the other party to act against his own wishes. This threat can be used similar to power in a negotiation. Rights are generally enforced through a third party such the courts or through arbitration or grievance procedures

Power is the ability to force someone to do something he would not otherwise do. Threatening to fire someone or to stop doing business with them are power moves.

It's important to be able to use interest, right or power moves to achieve you aims. Interest based dispute resolution is most likely to result in the best solution. Rights and power based solutions are adversarial and more expensive than interest based methods. Future prospects of dealing with the other party are diminished.

Chapter 10

Building Trust

In the early days of global exploration and trade, the crews of trading ships would leave a small quantity of trade goods on the beach of an inhabited island and then sail away. They would return the next day to see if anything had been left in return. If their trade goods had not been taken, or if they were taken and nothing was left in return, they would sail away in search of better prospects. They had left only a small quantity of goods, therefore, their risk was also small.

If the trade goods were gone and something valuable had been left in their place, larger and larger quantities of trade goods were left, encouraging larger and larger quantities of valuables in return.

In time, the natives would leave valuables first, expecting the traders to leave trade goods in return. In this way, trust was built between the traders and the natives. A small risk was taken in hopes of a small trade. The negotiators in these trades may never have talked or even seen each other, but they were building each other's trust, a little at a time.

Trust between the trader and the natives was based on experience and the prospect of mutual gain. Both parties benefited from the ongoing series of deals and didn't want it to end.

If someone wanted to consider using a new supplier, he might start out with a small order. If the quality, delivery and other important aspects of the order were satisfactory, he might try a larger order. As trust was established between the business and its supplier, larger orders would ensue. As long as the business and its supplier continue to enjoy mutual benefit from their dealings, trust would grow.

In time, such dealings can result in what amounts to a strategic partnership. Each party will be vested in the other's success. Each party will know what is expected of it and can be relied on to do it. Both parties can be counted on to help the other if he is in a bind. Trust is built on experience and mutual interest. Sometimes the experience is someone else's experience. If someone recommends a lawyer, accountant, supplier or a client because they were happy with their work, you would be more likely to trust them to do a good job for you too.

The Negotiator's Dilemma

The negotiator's dilemma has to do with whether you compete or cooperate with your negotiating counterpart. Cooperating requires more disclosure of information than competing and relies on your counterpart to cooperate and disclose information too. But if you divulge information and your counterpart doesn't, you may well find yourself at a disadvantage.

For example, a small appliance maker, Jones & Company, receives a substantial order for toaster ovens from a large, multinational, retail store chain. The appliance manufacturer can cope with the order by adding a second shift, but its regular suppliers of heating elements are booked up for months in advance and have no excess capacity. Without a supply of heating elements this order for toaster ovens might not be fulfilled and Jones & Co.' s opportunity to get their foot in the door with this retail giant might be lost.

A buyer for the toaster oven company finds a manufacturer of heating elements, Smith Enterprises, in another state. The manufacturer of heating elements has the machinery and capacity to make the heating elements.

Jones & Co. needs the heating elements to fulfill the largest order they have ever had. It is a chance to achieve the large, widespread distribution that they have long wanted. It might put them at a disadvantage in negotiations if Smith Enterprises knew how badly they needed the heating elements. Smith Enterprises would certainly have Jones & Co. over a barrel and could charge a much higher price than otherwise.

Smith Enterprises is losing money. It is on the verge of laying off more than half the workforce because of lack of business. If Jones & Co new this they could negotiate the purchase of its needed heater elements at rock bottom prices.

If Smith Enterprises knew of Jones & Co.'s difficulties, but kept its own predicament a secret, it would have a considerable advantage over Jones & Co.

If Jones & Co. knew of Smith Enterprises' precarious financial state, but kept its own difficulty a secret, it would have a substantial advantage over Smith Enterprises.

There are four possible outcomes to the dilemma. In terms of one's own perspective

Great If you compete, but the other negotiator tries to cooperate by divulging all pertinent information, you have the advantage. Your outcome will be great. The other negotiator's outcome will be terrible.

Good If you and your counterpart both disclose all the useful information to each other, you can cooperate and find mutually beneficial solutions. Both parties will have a good outcome.

Mediocre If neither party takes a cooperative role in disclosing information both parties will compete and end up splitting the pie and not creating any new value.

Awful If you try to cooperate, divulging information to your counterpart, spilling your negotiating guts, but you counterpart doesn't reciprocate, you lose. The other guy gets a great outcome, but yours is terrible.

Jones and Smith both need each other, though neither one realizes it. Both parties are reluctant to share too much information.

If Jones & Co. and Smith Enterprises can find a way to cooperate, they can both expect a good outcome. This is especially important if both companies expect to do business with each other in the future.

Quid Pro Quo

The Quid Pro Quo (this for that) or "tit for tat" strategy is usually the most successful at solving the negotiator's dilemma. It involves shared, careful, and incremental information disclosure. One negotiator starts with a cooperative tactic. He reveals a small bit of information about his interests. Next, he requests a similar revelation about his counterpart's interests. As the negotiations continue, he responds to a cooperative move with a cooperative move and to a competitive move with a competitive move.

It's hoped that cooperation will be the prevailing strategy and that every cooperative movement will be met with similar cooperation. This reciprocity will build an atmosphere of trust, leading both sides to reveal their interests candidly. The shared information will enable the creation of mutual advantage.

If a negotiator opens with a cooperative move only to be met with a competitive move, his next move should mirror his counterpart's move, tit for tat. Reply to a cooperative move with a cooperative move and a competitive move with a competitive move.

Most negotiators will quickly get the idea that if they want cooperation, they will have to give cooperation. If your counterpart does not start cooperating, at least you won't have given away the farm. The negotiation results won't be as good as they might have been, but you haven’t given the other negotiator the upper hand in what turned out to be a competitive, distributive, negotiation.

Chapter 11

Ploys, Gambits, and Dirty Tricks

Where do you draw the line? When does a simple negotiating ploy become a dirty trick? It's hard to say exactly where to draw the line sometimes. Some things always qualify as dirty tricks. Lying, cheating and stealing would come under the heading of dirty tricks. Bluffing is within the rules. Chester Karrass, an expert on ploys in negotiating, says that negotiation is like poker. Bluffing is allowed. You don't need to reveal your intentions too early. But, you can't open with less than a pair of jacks or keep an ace up your sleeve. Be careful with bluffing though. It's easy to go over the line into outright misrepresentation. There is also the possibility that your counterpart might call your bluff.

While it's good to be a strong negotiator, you don't want to take unfair advantage of anyone. You don't want anyone to regret doing business with you. Word would get around and nobody will want to do deal with you. The people you took unfair advantage of don't just disappear, they can reappear at the most inopportune moment and your dirty dealings can come back to bite you.

When in doubt about whether your actions cross the line into the unethical side, think about this; would your mother approve of what you're doing?

Ploys

A ploy is an action, often indirect, designed to turn a situation to one's own advantage. Sometimes ploys work, but only sometimes. Our goal here is to expose some of the most common ploys. If you recognize a ploy, it can often be defused simply by exposing it.

"Oh, I see, the old 'Good Cop, Bad Cop routine,' is it?" A comment like that will neutralize the ploy. It might make them feel a bit silly for even trying it.

Preconditions

Preconditions are often an attempt to gain an advantage even before negotiations start. If you don't accept the preconditions, negotiations will never begin.

Sometimes preconditions are confidence building measures. The willingness to accept them is sometimes the jump start needed to get negotiations started. It may lead the parties to accept negotiation as a road to solving their problems. Remember that we don't give anything away, we trade for it. Make it clear that you'll want something in return for accepting the preconditions, either you own preconditions or something you want when negotiations start.

Often, especially if stated loudly and publicly, preconditions are only a just a way to stage a propaganda war. This kind of blustering is likely to only make the situation more difficult.

Nonnegotiable Issues

Nonnegotiable issues are similar to preconditions in many ways. The intention is to limit negotiations, and gain an advantage without negotiating. If the demand for certain issues to be nonnegotiable includes matters that are of importance to you, it may block the deal.

You can agree to set aside the issues that your counterpart considers nonnegotiable, and see if progress can be made elsewhere. Your counterpart may find enough benefit is available in a deal that he may become more flexible in terms of what is negotiable. You may be able to get enough of what you want that you may be willing to concede on the nonnegotiable issues. Either way, nonnegotiable issues will make any dealings more difficult.

On occasion, the party you're dealing with may have the power to impose nonnegotiable conditions on you. For instance, if you're dealing with the IRS, negotiations might be useful on some matters, but you can't negotiate the tax laws.

Funny Money

Using funny money involves stating costs in a way that hides the amount of money involved. Car salesmen tell you that "you can drive that new car for only $385 per month." No mention is made of the actual price, how many payments would be needed or even if you would own the car at the end of the payments. Some car dealers have gotten in trouble for leasing cars to unsuspecting customers who thought they were buying the car.

Dividing costs into units that sound insignificant, doesn't *make* them insignificant. There is one grocery chain that advertises the price of their steaks at 10 ounce increments. The price looks good if you don't read the fine print that you only get 10 ounces for that price. Most meat is priced by the pound and our brain is used to comparing prices that way. Shady retailers intentionally make it hard to comparison shop.

"Would you like the three year extended warranty on your new television? It's only 49 cents a day." Gee, that sounds like cheap insurance for your new $600 TV. But if you add it up it comes to $536.55. It's not so cheap when do the math. Do the math.

Some negotiators will use the same kind of funny money ploys on you when you negotiate. They will try to obscure real costs by using units of measure that things look cheaper. Always translate into usable units before you continue to negotiate. And always read the fine print.

The Wince or Flinch

This is one of the oldest ploys in the book. Upon hearing an offer or proposal, flinch, look surprised, even shocked. You facial expression should convey the message "Heavens to Betsy!! You want how much!?"

The intention is to get a quick concession. It's surprising how many negotiators will immediately contemplate a concession when confronted with a flinch. Your counterpart may even start to defend his position

A practiced negotiator will usually start by offering the best terms that they think they can possibly get. They then observe your reaction and adjust their terms in view of that reaction. They don't expect to reach agreement on those terms, they just want to gauge the reaction. If you don't appear shocked, or if it looks like you are considering their terms, they will push for even more.

You should either suggest tactfully that he come up with a realistic offer, or counteroffer with an equally unrealistic offer in your favor, bracketing your goal price.

If you're on the receiving end of the flinch, ignore it. Assuming that your offer was reasonable, there's no need to acknowledge the look of shock on your counterparts face. Resist the urge to contemplate his acting ability. You opening offer should be in strongly your favor, but not completely unreasonable. There is no cause for the other negotiator to look surprised.

Good Cop, Bad Cop

You've seen this ploy a hundred times on TV. The police are interrogating a suspect. The bad cop yells, threatens, and acts aggressive and obnoxious. The good cop intervenes and saves the suspect from the bad cop. The good cop is now the suspect's friend and gets his full cooperation.

It works the same way during negotiations, except it's good negotiator, bad negotiator. The bad negotiator doesn't even have to exist. The negotiator may tell you that his boss is very difficult to deal with and that he'll try to intercede on your behalf. But you'll need to make some concessions if your new friend is going to have any chance of getting the deal by his boss.

One reason why this technique is often effective is that offers a way to comply, without making it seem they are giving in to a bully. The negotiator may meet the terms of the good negotiator simply to show the bully that his tactics don’t work, but being pleasant does.

If the bad cop negotiator is the boss, you can try to insist on talking to him directly, but he may not really exist

You can defuse this ploy pointing out that you know what they are doing. If they continue, they will just look and feel silly.

The Bogey

The bogey is a way of testing the asking price credibility of a product (or service.) It consists of telling the seller that you love his product, but your budget isn't enough to pay the asking price. It's hard to get upset at someone who really likes your product. If you haven't already told him, the seller will probably ask for the amount you are able to spend. Rather than simply walk away, he will try to find ways to make his product fit your budget.

It's unlikely that the seller will simply agree to sell at the price you have budgeted. But he will still look for ways to make the sale The seller knows more about his product than you do. He will go into detail about the virtues of his product,. He may offer details of his costs. He will be working with you to get the price down. He may help explore your needs and suggest lower cost possibilities.

He may simply lower the price on his product by dropping some options, changing the delivery schedule or by some other means.

If someone uses the bogey on you, test the bogey to see if there's any flexibility in it. You should also be ready to offer an alternative that matches the budget. This alternative may be sufficiently undesirable to make the buyer rethink his budget. You can also go over the buyer's head and deal with the person who sets the budget. Going over the buyer's head will usually offend the buyer, so this won't always be a good option if you're planning to do business with this person in the future.

The Crunch

"You've got to do better than that." That is all there is to the crunch. You are letting your counterpart know that his last offer is inadequate. Simple as it may be, this is a very effective tactic. If you're a buyer, it can often get the seller to lower his price.

If you are a seller, you can pad your prices to give yourself room to maneuver when dealing with someone who uses the crunch. That works best when you know that a particular buyer is going to use the crunch.

Ask questions. Why does the buyer think the price is too high? What price did they expect? Defend your price. What if the buyer still insists it's too high? Perhaps the price could be reduced by lowering the quantity or the quality, or adjusting the delivery schedule.

The Nibble (before final agreement)

The negotiator adds a small item after the deal after both parties have spent significant time and effort and the deal seems all but done. "I really like the car, and the price is O.K. If you can throw in the upgraded stereo that we talked about, I'll buy it now." The nibble is small in comparison to the whole agreement.

Remember that your counterpart also has an investment in time and effort and is unlikely to let this nibble interfere with the deal. Look surprised. Say something like "Gee, I thought we already covered everything." Ask if there is anything else before the deal is finalized. Remember, a good negotiator never gives anything away, he trades. Unless it's truly insignificant, ask for something in return. The nibbler may decide just forget the whole thing and stick with the agreement as it stands.

Salami

Salami is usually cut into slices before it is eaten. A negotiator will be more likely to make large concessions if they are cut into several small concessions. Matyas Rakosis, the former head of the Hungarian Communist party defined the salami ploy this way: "When you want to get hold of a salami sausage which your opponents are strenuously defending, you must not grab at it. You must start by carving yourself a very thin slice. The owner of the salami will hardly notice or, if he does, not mind very much. The next day you will carve another slice, and then still another. And so, little by little, the salami will pass into your possession."

When you're discussing a compensation package, don't blurt out everything you want all at once. Start with salary, then vacation days, and then flextime. Follow that with pension, personal days off and so on

If someone is using the salami ploy on you, the first defense is to recognize it. This ploy works because it's not always recognized until it's too late. Refuse to agree to any more concessions until the whole salami is on the table, so to speak. Ask if there is anything else that your counterpart wants to discuss as part of the negotiations. Once all the issues are out in the open, they can be negotiated in the usual way.

Lowballing or Highballing

A buyer opens with an unreasonably low price. Or a seller opens with an unreasonable high price. The opening price is completely out of the question and nobody really expects the transaction to take place at that price. Nevertheless, human psychology makes it difficult to totally ignore this number. The other negotiator is trying to use the unreasonable price as an anchor. If you let him get away with it, the ending price will probably be closer to the initial offer than it would have been otherwise.

Anchoring can be defused by recognizing it for what it is and insisting on starting negotiations at a more reasonable figure. Bracketing is another counter to anchoring with a lowball or highball figure. A counteroffer is made to an equal amount beyond your goal figure, but in the other direction. For instance, you want to buy a car and a reasonable goal price is $10,000. If the seller asks for $15,000, you might offer $5,000. Your offer is as much below your goal price as his is above. You are bracketing the price you hope to buy for. When haggling over a single issue, such as price, most negotiations end up somewhere near the middle of the opening figures.

Limited Authority

A negotiator who claims limited authority is often better off strategically then one who doesn't. A negotiator with limited authority can't be pressured into making a decision, but can gather information, test positions and explore possible trades. Such a negotiator can back a position by claiming that they only have authority to move just so far on a position and no farther. For instance, purchasers sometimes use the limited authority ploy by defining a range where they can make the deal and indicating that anything in excess of that amount requires the review and unlikely approval of a person or board with higher authority.

Just because your counterpart says "It's out of my hands." doesn't mean that's really the case. It may just be a bluff to gain tactical advantage. Your options include testing the limits of your counterpart. If it is a bluff, persistence may force the other negotiator to back down. You could also ask to deal directly with whoever it is that has the authority.

If company policy declares minimum order sizes, delivery charges, large deposits, maximum volume discounts or such, you can't expect the salesperson to be able to change them. You choice then is to deal within the constraints imposed or go somewhere else.

Escalating Authority

After an agreement appears to be reached, one of the negotiators announces that it's necessary to show the agreement to someone else for approval. This approval is often presented as routine matter. But, much to the negotiator's apparent surprise, the deal is rejected unless further concession are made. This ploy is almost universal among car salesman who must "run the deal past my manager."

If the deal is renegotiated, including the needed concessions, it may go through round after round of higher and higher authorities who reject the agreement unless more and more concessions are granted. These may be real or made up people with authority to approve the deal. Sometimes there are the imaginary bad cops to your counterpart's good cop.

When confronted with the escalating authority ploy, say something like "I understand, but you will recommend they accept, won't you?". Don't repeat your positions and their reasons at every level; let your counterpart do it.

If your counterpart leaves the room to get approval and comes back with the bad news that it wasn't approved, explain that you've been reexamining the deal and you can't really go through with it as proposed. You'll need just a few more concessions. This puts your counterpart in the position of having to defend the original agreement.

Split the Difference

Splitting the difference sounds fair. We all want to be fair don't we? Well, it might not be fair. The key here is to make sure that the midway position is favorable to you.

Try to get your counterpart to make the offer to split the difference. By making the offer they are, in effect, making a concession in the hope that you'll make a similar one. You don't necessarily want to do it. For instance, you're considering buying a store fixture. Your offer is $900 and the sales person has offered to sell it for $1000. You might point out that the difference is small. This may induce the seller to offer to split the difference. The seller has just lowered his price to $950, before you agreed to do the same. You reply "Yes, $950 is closer to what I can pay, but still a little high, $900 is what I had in mind. But if you can meet me halfway between the $950 you want and my price of $900, I'll go for it. Make it $925, and I'll write you a check right away." (Notice the condition/offer bargain) The difference has been split and then split again. In the end it's a 75/25 split.

If someone offers to split the difference with you, he has placed himself at a disadvantage by offering concession that you don't have to reciprocate equally. Ask yourself if the midpoint is reasonable or if you think you can do better.

The Quivering Pen

Also called "the quivering quill," this ploy has been around since well before the invention of modern writing implements. This ploy is similar to the nibble, but usually concerns changes in something already agreed to.

This is when the negotiator pauses, just before signing the agreement, possibly with his pen hovering over the paper, looks at his counterpart and asks for something more. "I'm still a little uncomfortable with the sales figures that we need to make before out volume discount kicks in. I would be more comfortable at 950 units rather than 1000. Can we change that?"

Just when you thought the deal was done. You've breathed a sigh of relief that the negotiations are finished, the feeling of pleasure that comes with the accomplishment of a job well done sets in. Then this person demands something else. What do you do? You might be tempted to give in and let them have what they want rather than start negotiations again. If you do this, you may find yourself being put on the spot again for another concession just before the pen hits the paper. This can go on repeatedly.

If the concession truly is insignificant, you can make sure that there are no more last minute concessions to deal with before the agreement is finalized. Several of these little concessions make one bigger concession and that's going to mean that negotiations are going to reopen. If the concession is significant, you're going to have to reopen negotiations anyway. You'll want something in return for the concession that they're asking for. Good negotiators never give anything away. They trade for it.

The Decoy

The negotiator makes a big deal about something that really doesn't matter in hopes of getting a concession on something else. "What? It doesn't come in blue? I really wanted it in blue. Well, can you at least give me free delivery if you can't get the color I want?" The truth is that nobody cares what color it is. Raising a fuss about an unimportant detail is a decoy, what's really wanted in this case is a lower price.

Red Herring

The red herring is similar to the Decoy. A negotiator lists a number of issues that he says are important. In truth, only some are important, others are included as red herring. They are negotiation fodder. The red herring are not important at all. They are there to give the negotiator something to concede in order to trade for a concession from his counterpart.

If negotiations are bogged down with a minor issue that your counterpart insists on settling before going on to other issues, either it's more than a minor issue or it's a red herring. Ask questions to try to discern which it is. Keep focused on the serious issues. You could offer a concession on an insignificant matter, in a sense trading a red herring for a red herring. In any case, don't let your counterpart link it to a concession you are disinclined to make.

Planted Information

One party to a negotiation allows the other party to "discover" information that hasn't been made available. This can be done by throwing a memo in the wastepaper basket during a break in negotiations. It can also be done by writing something in one's notes that is big and easy to read upside down. A note between members of a negotiating team can be left on the table during a break. There multitudes of ways to plant information or start rumors.

The other side is expected to trust this information more than what the negotiator is saying himself. It's human nature to trust what we learn ourselves more than what we're told, especially if it's private information. This private information may change the perceptions or expectations the party who found it.

The information 'found' might be something like "The price from XYZ corp. is $9000 lower." If a note between a buyer's negotiators with this information was read by the negotiators for a seller, it might encourage the seller to lower the price by $9500

The key to making this little ploy work is to make it seem as if the memo or note wasn't supposed to be discovered. Even so, the other negotiator might not take the bait

If you're the recipient of such information, seriously consider whether it was planted. Research the information as well as you can. If it's a rumor that you heard, you might save a lot of time and effort by simply asking your counterpart if the information is accurate or not. If they say it's true, ask them for the source of their information.

If you found the information by routing around in the waste paper basket, ignore it and don't do that anymore.

Gambits

A gambit is a device or action that is calculated to gain advantage. It is similar to a ploy but more direct. A gambit always entails a degree of risk.

Bluffing

A bluff consists of stating that positions are nonnegotiable when in fact they are negotiable. Bluffs also consist of warnings of adverse consequences that a negotiator might cause if he refuses to agree to certain terms, when in it is not really the case. Bluffing is common in negotiation because each side has limited information. A good bluff uses your counterpart's uncertainty to create even more doubt. Doubt turns into risk, and risk turns in to money. Be alert for signs of uncertainty in your counterpart's voice, expression or body language

If you are going to bluff, and take the risk of your bluff being called, keep these guidelines in mind

- Only bluff on important issues.
- Couple your bluff with flexibility on another issue. It will make it more credible.
- Support your bluff with a plausible reason.
- Ensure that you have an opportunity to back down if you counterpart calls your bluff. You can cite "New information" or "Changing conditions."

If you feel your counterpart is bluffing, one option is simply to call the bluff. The danger here is that the other negotiator may not be bluffing after all. Another, less direct, is to inquire into the reasons for the inflexibility about the particular issue. This may lead to a solution to the negotiation bottleneck and give the bluffing negotiator a way out without actually appearing to back down.

Take It or Leave It

A lot of business is conducted on a "take it or leave it" basis. When you go into a grocery store, the price of everything is marked. You can either pay the price or not buy the item. You are not going to be able to haggle with the store manager over the price of a can of soup.

Most of the negotiating you are going to do involves higher stakes than the price of a can of soup. If you are on the receiving end of this ultimatum, you have to decide if it is legitimate. If this ultimatum is given late in negotiations, after all avenues toward finding a better alternative have been explored, it is more likely to be real.

There are three ways of dealing with this ultimatum. The first way is to simply ignore it, continue as if you never heard it. This will test the seriousness of the demand. Focus on their needs and interests rather than on the demand. The second way is to question your counterpart about what he thinks will happen if an agreement is not made. Though the expression "Take it or leave it." implies indifference, it's likely that they would like you to take the deal. Negotiations can continue.

The final option is to take the ultimatum at face value. If negotiations are at an impasse, your counterpart may have nothing left to trade and no more concessions that can be made. Consider your BATNA. Are your alternatives better than accepting this deal? That is the key to deciding whether to take the deal as it is or to walk away.

If the situation is such that you are the one to offer this ultimatum, be careful of how you phrase it. If you just say "Take it or leave it." you will sound aggressive and confrontational. Your counterpart may decide to leave it rather than give in to your demands. It would be an emotional reaction, but not a surprising one.

A better way would be to explain to your counterpart in an almost apologetic tone that you have no more to give. You have reached the limit of the concessions that you can make. Tell them that what you have offered is the best that you can do for them and ask them to accept it.

Bluffing would be dangerous at this point. If they don't accept the deal as the best you can possibly give them, it would be difficult to restart negotiations.

Walking Out

If the other negotiator won't agree to your terms, you can just give up and walk out. There is no risk in this if you can get a better deal elsewhere. Keep your BATNA in mind

But what if your BATNA isn't better than the deal currently being offered? That's where the risk comes in. If you walk out on the deal, trying to get your counterpart to believe that you have a better deal waiting in the wings, he may just let you go. He may really be at the limit of what he is willing to concede to make the deal.

If you do this, be sure to end the negotiations on a civil tone. Explain that you enjoyed negotiating with them even though you couldn't make a deal. Give them a way to call you back to the negotiating table. Leave your phone number. Don't walk too quickly to the door.

If you are bluffing, leave yourself a way out. If it looks like your counterpart is going to let you walk, you can turn around just as you get to the door and say something like -" Your price is very close to your competitor. If I bought this machinery from you, could you include a few hours of instruction on the finer points of its maintenance?"

Dirty tricks

Bad Math

The bad math ploy depends on the victim's ethical lapse. The victim is presented with a written proposal or sales contract that deliberately omits or underprices one of the elements. Sometimes it's just a mathematical error in your favor. While the victim is rushing to take advantage of this windfall, he becomes a careless negotiator. This carelessness is taken advantage of. As the victim eagerly puts his pen to paper, the error is noticed and corrected.

The best way to counter this ploy is to point out the error as soon as you notice it. You could say something like "I assume that you're not charging me the higher total price because you're anxious for me to make a decision right away." Put the person trying this ploy on the defensive.

Fait Accompli

Someone takes an action as if an agreement has already been made, Examples include

- A repair shop fixes your car before agreement on price, not giving you the estimate that you asked for.
- A customer takes a discount for prompt payment, even though none was offered.
- A vender delivers merchandise after you ask for a price, but have not actually agreed to that price or placed an order.

Often, once the action is taken, it is difficult to undo. The idea is to circumvent negotiation completely. When they are caught, they will profess that it's an honest mistake, a simple case of misunderstanding your intentions. Your options here are to go to the effort to undo what they have done or to let it slide and save yourself the trouble.

Whichever you decide, it would be wise to avoid doing business with these scoundrels in the future if at all possible.

Brooklyn Camera Store

This ploy is named after some companies who sell cameras through an 800 number or on the internet. The camera is advertised at a very low price. Once you commit to buying the camera, you discover that it is a much stripped down model. It doesn't come with the accessories usually included with a camera. "Would you like a lens cap for that camera? It's only $5." Then of course there's the strap, a case, the manual and on and on. It's not exactly the old bait and switch, more like bait and accessorize.

The gist of this ploy is to break everything down into small packages and then negotiate them one at a time If selling, everything is priced separately. Once the main item is sold, show the extras that are needed. Any mention of the total cost is avoided until each individual item is agreed on.

Avoid this by asking what is included in the deal at the outset. Insist on a price for the whole package. Consider doing business somewhere else.

The Nibble (after agreement.)

Nibbling before an agreement is signed is one thing, nibbling after an agreement is another. Trying to slip in another concession or two before an agreement is concluded is sometimes annoying, but by no means unethical. Using the nibble after an agreement is downright shady. It consists of such things as:

- Taking discounts for prompt payment even though none was offered and the payment wasn't prompt.
- Delivering sub-standard parts to a manufacturer when it is too late do anything to remedy the situation.
- Sending orders that list one quantity on the invoice, but consist of fewer items.
- Placing an order large enough to get a volume discount, then calling to reduce the size of the order at the last moment, while insisting on keeping the volume discount.

When dealing with someone who you suspect is a post-negotiation nibbler, be sure to cover all the details of the agreement in writing. Better yet, avoid doing business with them completely.

These are people that you don't want to deal with. They may gain 2 or 3 percent advantage on these nibbles, but it will cost a fortune to keep an eagle eye on them to make sure they aren't cheating you. You'll have to count all orders to see if you've been shorted. You'll have to test quality to see if what you bought is up to the standards that you agreed on. You'll have to rebill to recover discounts taken that were not earned. A serious amount of time and effort will be spent routing out and protecting yourself from their shady shenanigans. You have better things to do than being constantly on guard, double checking everything and fixing what this unprincipled rascal has done.

Changing the Deal After the Deal

Car dealers are famous for this. Once you agree to a price, they'll try to sell you add-ons. Such as fancy wheels, a really nifty stereo that you just can't live without. That's simple salesmanship. But when you get ready to sign the papers, you may find other things added on. Taxes and registration fees are legit. Things like surprise "Dealer fees" or "Administrative fees" are not.

Ask up front at the beginning of any discussion what is included and what is not. Make it clear that you don't want any type of added charges at the last minute.

If you are presented with any of these surprise charges for things that should have been included in the purchase price; or were added later, you should start negotiations again from the beginning. Insist that all fees and charges be included in the negotiated price and that there be no surprises. Better yet, just walk away.

Visit

www.SmallBizNegotiation.com

www.ingramcontent.com/pod-product-compliance
Lightning Source LLC
LaVergne TN
LVHW020644100826
845148LV00012B/2337

* 9 7 8 0 6 1 5 7 9 6 6 2 8 *